# 2021
# 2022

Planner

# *Personal details*

Name  :

Phone :

Address :

Email  :

Fax  :

Bank account number N° :

Identity card N° :

Passeport N°:

Blood group :

Divers :

# Contact list :

| NAME | ADRESS | PHONE | MAIL |
| --- | --- | --- | --- |

# Contact list :

| NAME | ADRESS | PHONE | MAIL |
| --- | --- | --- | --- |

# Contact list :

| NAME | ADRESS | PHONE | MAIL |
|------|--------|-------|------|
|      |        |       |      |

May 2021

| | May 2021 | | | | | |
| --- | --- | --- | --- | --- | --- | --- |
| M | T | W | T | F | S | S |
| | | | | | 1 | 2 |
| 3 | 4 | 5 | 6 | 7 | 8 | 9 |
| 10 | 11 | 12 | 13 | 14 | 15 | 16 |
| 17 | 18 | 19 | 20 | 21 | 22 | 23 |
| 24 | 25 | 26 | 27 | 28 | 29 | 30 |
| 31 | | | | | | |

Mon **31**

.............. June 2021 ..................

Tue **1**

Wed **2**

# June 2021

Thu **3**

| June 2021 | | | | | | |
|---|---|---|---|---|---|---|
| **M** | **T** | **W** | **T** | **F** | **S** | **S** |
| | 1 | 2 | 3 | 4 | 5 | **6** |
| 7 | 8 | 9 | 10 | 11 | 12 | **13** |
| 14 | 15 | 16 | 17 | 18 | 19 | **20** |
| 21 | 22 | 23 | 24 | 25 | 26 | **27** |
| 28 | 29 | 30 | | | | |

Fri **4**

Sat **5**

Sun **6**

Mon **7**

Tue **8**

Wed **9**

June 2021

| **June 2021** | | | | | | |
|---|---|---|---|---|---|---|
| M | T | W | T | F | S | S |
|  | 1 | 2 | 3 | 4 | 5 | 6 |
| 7 | 8 | 9 | 10 | 11 | 12 | 13 |
| 14 | 15 | 16 | 17 | 18 | 19 | 20 |
| 21 | 22 | 23 | 24 | 25 | 26 | 27 |
| 28 | 29 | 30 |  |  |  |  |

Thu **10**

Fri **11**

Sat **12**

Sun **13**

June 2021

Mon **14**

Tue **15**

Wed **16**

June 2021

Thu **17**

| M | T | W | T | F | S | S |
|---|---|---|---|---|---|---|
| **June 2021** | | | | | | |
|  | 1 | 2 | 3 | 4 | 5 | 6 |
| 7 | 8 | 9 | 10 | 11 | 12 | 13 |
| 14 | 15 | 16 | 17 | 18 | 19 | 20 |
| 21 | 22 | 23 | 24 | 25 | 26 | 27 |
| 28 | 29 | 30 |  |  |  |  |

Fri **18**

Sat **19**

Sun **20**

Mon **21**

Tue **22**

Wed **23**

June 2021

Thu **24**

Fri **25**

Sat **26**

Sun **27**

| June 2021 | | | | | | |
|---|---|---|---|---|---|---|
| M | T | W | T | F | S | S |
| | 1 | 2 | 3 | 4 | 5 | 6 |
| 7 | 8 | 9 | 10 | 11 | 12 | 13 |
| 14 | 15 | 16 | 17 | 18 | 19 | 20 |
| 21 | 22 | 23 | 24 | 25 | 26 | 27 |
| 28 | 29 | 30 | | | | |

June 2021

Mon **28**

<table>
<tr><td colspan="7" align="center">**June 2021**</td></tr>
<tr><td>M</td><td>T</td><td>W</td><td>T</td><td>F</td><td>S</td><td>S</td></tr>
<tr><td></td><td>1</td><td>2</td><td>3</td><td>4</td><td>5</td><td>6</td></tr>
<tr><td>7</td><td>8</td><td>9</td><td>10</td><td>11</td><td>12</td><td>13</td></tr>
<tr><td>14</td><td>15</td><td>16</td><td>17</td><td>18</td><td>19</td><td>20</td></tr>
<tr><td>21</td><td>22</td><td>23</td><td>24</td><td>25</td><td>26</td><td>27</td></tr>
<tr><td>28</td><td>29</td><td>30</td><td></td><td></td><td></td><td></td></tr>
</table>

Tue **29**

Wed **30**

July 2021

| | July 2021 | | | | | |
|---|---|---|---|---|---|---|
| **M** | **T** | **W** | **T** | **F** | **S** | **S** |
| | | | 1 | 2 | 3 | **4** |
| 5 | 6 | 7 | 8 | 9 | 10 | **11** |
| 12 | 13 | 14 | 15 | 16 | 17 | **18** |
| 19 | 20 | 21 | 22 | 23 | 24 | **25** |
| 26 | 27 | 28 | 29 | 30 | 31 | |

Thu **1**

Fri **2**

Sat **3**

Sun **4**

# July 2021

Mon **5**

Tue **6**

Wed **7**

July 2021

Thu **8**

| July 2021 | | | | | | |
|---|---|---|---|---|---|---|
| M | T | W | T | F | S | S |
|  |  |  | 1 | 2 | 3 | 4 |
| 5 | 6 | 7 | 8 | 9 | 10 | 11 |
| 12 | 13 | 14 | 15 | 16 | 17 | 18 |
| 19 | 20 | 21 | 22 | 23 | 24 | 25 |
| 26 | 27 | 28 | 29 | 30 | 31 |  |

Fri **9**

Sat **10**

Sun **11**

Mon **12**

Tue **13**

Wed **14**

July 2021

Thu **15**

Fri **16**

Sat **17**

Sun **18**

Mon **19**

Tue **20**

Wed **21**

July 2021

Thu **22**

---

Fri **23**

---

Sat **24**

Sun **25**

| July 2021 | | | | | | |
|---|---|---|---|---|---|---|
| M | T | W | T | F | S | S |
|  |  |  | 1 | 2 | 3 | 4 |
| 5 | 6 | 7 | 8 | 9 | 10 | 11 |
| 12 | 13 | 14 | 15 | 16 | 17 | 18 |
| 19 | 20 | 21 | 22 | 23 | 24 | 25 |
| 26 | 27 | 28 | 29 | 30 | 31 |  |

Mon **26**

Tue **27**

Wed **28**

July 2021

Thu **29**

Fri **30**

Sat **31**

....... August 2021 ......

Sun **1**

| | July 2021 | | | | | |
|---|---|---|---|---|---|---|
| **M** | **T** | **W** | **T** | **F** | **S** | **S** |
| | | | 1 | 2 | 3 | **4** |
| 5 | 6 | 7 | 8 | 9 | 10 | **11** |
| 12 | 13 | 14 | 15 | 16 | 17 | **18** |
| 19 | 20 | 21 | 22 | 23 | 24 | **25** |
| 26 | 27 | 28 | 29 | 30 | 31 | |

# August 2021

Mon **2**

Tue **3**

Wed **4**

August 2021

| | August 2021 | | | | | |
|---|---|---|---|---|---|---|
| M | T | W | T | F | S | S |
| | | | | | | 1 |
| 2 | 3 | 4 | 5 | 6 | 7 | 8 |
| 9 | 10 | 11 | 12 | 13 | 14 | 15 |
| 16 | 17 | 18 | 19 | 20 | 21 | 22 |
| 23 | 24 | 25 | 26 | 27 | 28 | 29 |
| 30 | 31 | | | | | |

Thu **5**

Fri **6**

Sat **7**

Sun **8**

August 2021

Mon **9**

Tue **10**

Wed **11**

## August 2021

| | August 2021 | | | | | |
| M | T | W | T | F | S | S |
|---|---|---|---|---|---|---|
| | | | | | | 1 |
| 2 | 3 | 4 | 5 | 6 | 7 | 8 |
| 9 | 10 | 11 | 12 | 13 | 14 | 15 |
| 16 | 17 | 18 | 19 | 20 | 21 | 22 |
| 23 | 24 | 25 | 26 | 27 | 28 | 29 |
| 30 | 31 | | | | | |

Thu **12**

Fri **13**

Sat **14**

Sun **15**

Mon **16**

Tue **17**

Wed **18**

# August 2021

| August 2021 | | | | | | |
|---|---|---|---|---|---|---|
| **M** | **T** | **W** | **T** | **F** | **S** | **S** |
| | | | | | | **1** |
| 2 | 3 | 4 | 5 | 6 | 7 | **8** |
| 9 | 10 | 11 | 12 | 13 | 14 | **15** |
| 16 | 17 | 18 | 19 | 20 | 21 | **22** |
| 23 | 24 | 25 | 26 | 27 | 28 | **29** |
| 30 | 31 | | | | | |

Thu **19**

Fri **20**

Sat **21**

Sun **22**

Mon **23**

Tue **24**

Wed **25**

## August 2021

<table>
<tr><td colspan="8">August 2021</td></tr>
<tr><td>M</td><td>T</td><td>W</td><td>T</td><td>F</td><td>S</td><td>S</td></tr>
<tr><td></td><td></td><td></td><td></td><td></td><td></td><td>1</td></tr>
<tr><td>2</td><td>3</td><td>4</td><td>5</td><td>6</td><td>7</td><td>8</td></tr>
<tr><td>9</td><td>10</td><td>11</td><td>12</td><td>13</td><td>14</td><td>15</td></tr>
<tr><td>16</td><td>17</td><td>18</td><td>19</td><td>20</td><td>21</td><td>22</td></tr>
<tr><td>23</td><td>24</td><td>25</td><td>26</td><td>27</td><td>28</td><td>29</td></tr>
<tr><td>30</td><td>31</td><td></td><td></td><td></td><td></td><td></td></tr>
</table>

Thu **26**

Fri **27**

Sat **28**

Sun **29**

| | August 2021 | | | | | |
|---|---|---|---|---|---|---|
| **M** | **T** | **W** | **T** | **F** | **S** | **S** |
| | | | | | | 1 |
| 2 | 3 | 4 | 5 | 6 | 7 | 8 |
| 9 | 10 | 11 | 12 | 13 | 14 | 15 |
| 16 | 17 | 18 | 19 | 20 | 21 | 22 |
| 23 | 24 | 25 | 26 | 27 | 28 | 29 |
| 30 | 31 | | | | | |

Mon **30**

Tue **31**

·············· September 2021 ···············

Wed **1**

# September 2021

Thu **2**

| | September 2021 | | | | | | |
|---|---|---|---|---|---|---|---|
| **M** | **T** | **W** | **T** | **F** | **S** | **S** |
| | | 1 | 2 | 3 | 4 | **5** |
| 6 | 7 | 8 | 9 | 10 | 11 | **12** |
| 13 | 14 | 15 | 16 | 17 | 18 | **19** |
| 20 | 21 | 22 | 23 | 24 | 25 | **26** |
| 27 | 28 | 29 | 30 | | | |

Fri **3**

Sat **4**

Sun **5**

Mon **6**

Tue **7**

Wed **8**

## September 2021

**Thu 9**

| | September 2021 | | | | | |
|---|---|---|---|---|---|---|
| M | T | W | T | F | S | S |
| | | 1 | 2 | 3 | 4 | 5 |
| 6 | 7 | 8 | 9 | 10 | 11 | 12 |
| 13 | 14 | 15 | 16 | 17 | 18 | 19 |
| 20 | 21 | 22 | 23 | 24 | 25 | 26 |
| 27 | 28 | 29 | 30 | | | |

**Fri 10**

**Sat 11**

**Sun 12**

Mon **13**

Tue **14**

Wed **15**

## September 2021

Thu **16**

| September 2021 | | | | | | |
|---|---|---|---|---|---|---|
| M | T | W | T | F | S | S |
|  |  | 1 | 2 | 3 | 4 | 5 |
| 6 | 7 | 8 | 9 | 10 | 11 | 12 |
| 13 | 14 | 15 | 16 | 17 | 18 | 19 |
| 20 | 21 | 22 | 23 | 24 | 25 | 26 |
| 27 | 28 | 29 | 30 |  |  |  |

Fri **17**

Sat **18**

Sun **19**

Mon **20**

Tue **21**

Wed **22**

September 2021

Thu **23**

| | September 2021 | | | | | | |
|---|---|---|---|---|---|---|---|
| **M** | **T** | **W** | **T** | **F** | **S** | **S** |
| | | 1 | 2 | 3 | 4 | 5 |
| 6 | 7 | 8 | 9 | 10 | 11 | 12 |
| 13 | 14 | 15 | 16 | 17 | 18 | 19 |
| 20 | 21 | 22 | 23 | 24 | 25 | 26 |
| 27 | 28 | 29 | 30 | | | |

Fri **24**

Sat **25**

Sun **26**

Mon **27**

Tue **28**

Wed **29**

## September 2021

Thu **30**

| | September 2021 | | | | | | |
|---|---|---|---|---|---|---|
| **M** | **T** | **W** | **T** | **F** | **S** | **S** |
| | | 1 | 2 | 3 | 4 | **5** |
| 6 | 7 | 8 | 9 | 10 | 11 | **12** |
| 13 | 14 | 15 | 16 | 17 | 18 | **19** |
| 20 | 21 | 22 | 23 | 24 | 25 | **26** |
| 27 | 28 | 29 | 30 | | | |

.................…. October 2021 ...................…..

Fri **1**

Sat **2**

Sun **3**

Mon **4**

Tue **5**

Wed **6**

# October 2021

Thu **7**

Fri **8**

Sat **9**

Sun **10**

| October 2021 | | | | | | |
|---|---|---|---|---|---|---|
| M | T | W | T | F | S | S |
|  |  |  |  | 1 | 2 | 3 |
| 4 | 5 | 6 | 7 | 8 | 9 | 10 |
| 11 | 12 | 13 | 14 | 15 | 16 | 17 |
| 18 | 19 | 20 | 21 | 22 | 23 | 24 |
| 25 | 26 | 27 | 28 | 29 | 30 | 31 |

Mon **11**

Tue **12**

Wed **13**

October 2021

Thu **14**

| October 2021 | | | | | | |
| M | T | W | T | F | S | S |
| --- | --- | --- | --- | --- | --- | --- |
|  |  |  |  | 1 | 2 | 3 |
| 4 | 5 | 6 | 7 | 8 | 9 | 10 |
| 11 | 12 | 13 | 14 | 15 | 16 | 17 |
| 18 | 19 | 20 | 21 | 22 | 23 | 24 |
| 25 | 26 | 27 | 28 | 29 | 30 | 31 |

Fri **15**

Sat **16**

Sun **17**

Mon **18**

Tue **19**

Wed **20**

# October 2021

Thu **21**

Fri **22**

Sat **23**

Sun **24**

| October 2021 | | | | | | |
|---|---|---|---|---|---|---|
| M | T | W | T | F | S | S |
|  |  |  |  | 1 | 2 | 3 |
| 4 | 5 | 6 | 7 | 8 | 9 | 10 |
| 11 | 12 | 13 | 14 | 15 | 16 | 17 |
| 18 | 19 | 20 | 21 | 22 | 23 | 24 |
| 25 | 26 | 27 | 28 | 29 | 30 | 31 |

Mon **25**

Tue **26**

Wed **27**

October 2021

Thu **28**

| | October 2021 | | | | | |
|---|---|---|---|---|---|---|
| M | T | W | T | F | S | S |
| | | | | 1 | 2 | 3 |
| 4 | 5 | 6 | 7 | 8 | 9 | 10 |
| 11 | 12 | 13 | 14 | 15 | 16 | 17 |
| 18 | 19 | 20 | 21 | 22 | 23 | 24 |
| 25 | 26 | 27 | 28 | 29 | 30 | 31 |

Fri **29**

Sat **30**

Sun **31**

## November 2021

Mon **1**

Tue **2**

Wed **3**

# November 2021

| | November 2021 | | | | | |
|---|---|---|---|---|---|---|
| M | T | W | T | F | S | S |
| 1 | 2 | 3 | 4 | 5 | 6 | 7 |
| 8 | 9 | 10 | 11 | 12 | 13 | 14 |
| 15 | 16 | 17 | 18 | 19 | 20 | 21 |
| 22 | 23 | 24 | 25 | 26 | 27 | 28 |
| 29 | 30 | | | | | |

Thu **4**

Fri **5**

Sat **6**

Sun **7**

Mon **8**

Tue **9**

Wed **10**

# November 2021

Thu **11**

| November 2021 | | | | | | |
|---|---|---|---|---|---|---|
| **M** | **T** | **W** | **T** | **F** | **S** | **S** |
| 1 | 2 | 3 | 4 | 5 | 6 | **7** |
| 8 | 9 | 10 | 11 | 12 | 13 | **14** |
| 15 | 16 | 17 | 18 | 19 | 20 | **21** |
| 22 | 23 | 24 | 25 | 26 | 27 | **28** |
| 29 | 30 | | | | | |

Fri **12**

Sat **13**

Sun **14**

Mon **15**

Tue **16**

Wed **17**

November 2021

Thu **18**

| | November 2021 | | | | | |
|---|---|---|---|---|---|---|
| **M** | **T** | **W** | **T** | **F** | **S** | **S** |
| 1 | 2 | 3 | 4 | 5 | 6 | **7** |
| 8 | 9 | 10 | 11 | 12 | 13 | **14** |
| 15 | 16 | 17 | 18 | 19 | 20 | **21** |
| 22 | 23 | 24 | 25 | 26 | 27 | **28** |
| 29 | 30 | | | | | |

Fri **19**

Sat **20**

Sun **21**

Mon **22**

Tue **23**

Wed **24**

November 2021

Thu **25**

| | | November 2021 | | | | |
|---|---|---|---|---|---|---|
| **M** | **T** | **W** | **T** | **F** | **S** | **S** |
| 1 | 2 | 3 | 4 | 5 | 6 | 7 |
| 8 | 9 | 10 | 11 | 12 | 13 | 14 |
| 15 | 16 | 17 | 18 | 19 | 20 | 21 |
| 22 | 23 | 24 | 25 | 26 | 27 | 28 |
| 29 | 30 | | | | | |

Fri **26**

Sat **27**

Sun **28**

November 2021

Mon **29**



Tue **30**

............... December 2021 ...............

Wed **1**

# December 2021

**Thu 2**

**Fri 3**

**Sat 4**

**Sun 5**

| December 2021 | | | | | | |
|---|---|---|---|---|---|---|
| M | T | W | T | F | S | S |
|  |  | 1 | 2 | 3 | 4 | 5 |
| 6 | 7 | 8 | 9 | 10 | 11 | 12 |
| 13 | 14 | 15 | 16 | 17 | 18 | 19 |
| 20 | 21 | 22 | 23 | 24 | 25 | 26 |
| 27 | 28 | 29 | 30 | 31 |  |  |

# December 2021

### Mon 6

### Tue 7

### Wed 8

## December 2021

Thu **9**

| | December 2021 | | | | | | |
|---|---|---|---|---|---|---|---|
| **M** | **T** | **W** | **T** | **F** | **S** | **S** |
| | | 1 | 2 | 3 | 4 | 5 |
| 6 | 7 | 8 | 9 | 10 | 11 | 12 |
| 13 | 14 | 15 | 16 | 17 | 18 | 19 |
| 20 | 21 | 22 | 23 | 24 | 25 | 26 |
| 27 | 28 | 29 | 30 | 31 | | |

Fri **10**

Sat **11**

Sun **12**

Mon **13**

Tue **14**

Wed **15**

December 2021

Thu **16**

Fri **17**

Sat **18**

Sun **19**

| December 2021 | | | | | | |
|---|---|---|---|---|---|---|
| M | T | W | T | F | S | S |
|  |  | 1 | 2 | 3 | 4 | 5 |
| 6 | 7 | 8 | 9 | 10 | 11 | 12 |
| 13 | 14 | 15 | 16 | 17 | 18 | 19 |
| 20 | 21 | 22 | 23 | 24 | 25 | 26 |
| 27 | 28 | 29 | 30 | 31 |  |  |

Mon **20**

Tue **21**

Wed **22**

December 2021

Thu **23**

Fri **24**

Sat **25**

Sun **26**

| December 2021 | | | | | | |
|---|---|---|---|---|---|---|
| M | T | W | T | F | S | S |
|  |  | 1 | 2 | 3 | 4 | 5 |
| 6 | 7 | 8 | 9 | 10 | 11 | 12 |
| 13 | 14 | 15 | 16 | 17 | 18 | 19 |
| 20 | 21 | 22 | 23 | 24 | 25 | 26 |
| 27 | 28 | 29 | 30 | 31 |  |  |

Mon **27**

Tue **28**

Wed **29**

December 2021

Thu **30**

| December 2021 | | | | | | |
|---|---|---|---|---|---|---|
| M | T | W | T | F | S | S |
|  |  | 1 | 2 | 3 | 4 | 5 |
| 6 | 7 | 8 | 9 | 10 | 11 | 12 |
| 13 | 14 | 15 | 16 | 17 | 18 | 19 |
| 20 | 21 | 22 | 23 | 24 | 25 | 26 |
| 27 | 28 | 29 | 30 | 31 |  |  |

Fri **31**

# 2022

Planner

January 2022

Sat **1**

| | | January 2022 | | | | |
|---|---|---|---|---|---|---|
| **M** | **T** | **W** | **T** | **F** | **S** | **S** |
| | | | | | 1 | **2** |
| 3 | 4 | 5 | 6 | 7 | 8 | **9** |
| 10 | 11 | 12 | 13 | 14 | 15 | **16** |
| 17 | 18 | 19 | 20 | 21 | 22 | **23** |
| 24 | 25 | 26 | 27 | 28 | 29 | **30** |
| 31 | | | | | | |

Sun **2**

Mon **3**

Tue **4**

Wed **5**

# January 2022

Thu **6**

---

Fri **7**

---

| January 2022 | | | | | | |
|---|---|---|---|---|---|---|
| M | T | W | T | F | S | S |
|  |  |  |  |  | 1 | 2 |
| 3 | 4 | 5 | 6 | 7 | 8 | 9 |
| 10 | 11 | 12 | 13 | 14 | 15 | 16 |
| 17 | 18 | 19 | 20 | 21 | 22 | 23 |
| 24 | 25 | 26 | 27 | 28 | 29 | 30 |
| 31 |  |  |  |  |  |  |

---

Sat **8**

Sun **9**

Mon **10**

Tue **11**

Wed **12**

January 2022

Thu **13**

| | January 2022 | | | | | |
|---|---|---|---|---|---|---|
| M | T | W | T | F | S | S |
| | | | | | 1 | 2 |
| 3 | 4 | 5 | 6 | 7 | 8 | 9 |
| 10 | 11 | 12 | 13 | 14 | 15 | 16 |
| 17 | 18 | 19 | 20 | 21 | 22 | 23 |
| 24 | 25 | 26 | 27 | 28 | 29 | 30 |
| 31 | | | | | | |

Fri **14**

Sat **15**

Sun **16**

Mon **17**

Tue **18**

Wed **19**

January 2022

| | January 2022 | | | | | |
|---|---|---|---|---|---|---|
| M | T | W | T | F | S | S |
| | | | | | 1 | 2 |
| 3 | 4 | 5 | 6 | 7 | 8 | 9 |
| 10 | 11 | 12 | 13 | 14 | 15 | 16 |
| 17 | 18 | 19 | 20 | 21 | 22 | 23 |
| 24 | 25 | 26 | 27 | 28 | 29 | 30 |
| 31 | | | | | | |

Thu **20**

Fri **21**

Sat **22**

Sun **23**

Mon **24**

Tue **25**

Wed **26**

January 2022

Thu **27**

| January 2022 | | | | | | |
|---|---|---|---|---|---|---|
| M | T | W | T | F | S | S |
| | | | | | 1 | 2 |
| 3 | 4 | 5 | 6 | 7 | 8 | 9 |
| 10 | 11 | 12 | 13 | 14 | 15 | 16 |
| 17 | 18 | 19 | 20 | 21 | 22 | 23 |
| 24 | 25 | 26 | 27 | 28 | 29 | 30 |
| 31 | | | | | | |

Fri **28**

Sat **29**

Sun **30**

January 2022

Mon **31**



........... February 2022 ...........

Tue **1**

Wed **2**

February 2022

Thu **3**

| | | **February 2022** | | | | |
|---|---|---|---|---|---|---|
| **M** | **T** | **W** | **T** | **F** | **S** | **S** |
| | 1 | 2 | 3 | 4 | 5 | **6** |
| 7 | 8 | 9 | 10 | 11 | 12 | **13** |
| 14 | 15 | 16 | 17 | 18 | 19 | **20** |
| 21 | 22 | 23 | 24 | 25 | 26 | **27** |
| 28 | | | | | | |

Fri **4**

Sat **5**

Sun **6**

Mon **7**

Tue **8**

Wed **9**

February 2022

Thu **10**

| **February 2022** | | | | | | |
|---|---|---|---|---|---|---|
| M | T | W | T | F | S | S |
|  | 1 | 2 | 3 | 4 | 5 | 6 |
| 7 | 8 | 9 | 10 | 11 | 12 | 13 |
| 14 | 15 | 16 | 17 | 18 | 19 | 20 |
| 21 | 22 | 23 | 24 | 25 | 26 | 27 |
| 28 |  |  |  |  |  |  |

Fri **11**

Sat **12**

Sun **13**

February 2022

Mon **14**

Tue **15**

Wed **16**

February 2022

Thu **17**

<table>
<tr><td colspan="7" align="center">**February 2022**</td></tr>
<tr><td>M</td><td>T</td><td>W</td><td>T</td><td>F</td><td>S</td><td>S</td></tr>
<tr><td></td><td>1</td><td>2</td><td>3</td><td>4</td><td>5</td><td>6</td></tr>
<tr><td>7</td><td>8</td><td>9</td><td>10</td><td>11</td><td>12</td><td>13</td></tr>
<tr><td>14</td><td>15</td><td>16</td><td>17</td><td>18</td><td>19</td><td>20</td></tr>
<tr><td>21</td><td>22</td><td>23</td><td>24</td><td>25</td><td>26</td><td>27</td></tr>
<tr><td>28</td><td></td><td></td><td></td><td></td><td></td><td></td></tr>
</table>

Fri **18**

Sat **19**

Sun **20**

Mon **21**

Tue **22**

Wed **23**

February 2022

Thu **24**

| February 2022 | | | | | | |
|---|---|---|---|---|---|---|
| **M** | **T** | **W** | **T** | **F** | **S** | **S** |
|  | 1 | 2 | 3 | 4 | 5 | **6** |
| 7 | 8 | 9 | 10 | 11 | 12 | **13** |
| 14 | 15 | 16 | 17 | 18 | 19 | **20** |
| 21 | 22 | 23 | 24 | 25 | 26 | **27** |
| 28 |  |  |  |  |  |  |

Fri **25**

Sat **26**

Sun **27**

# February 2022



---

……… March 2022 ………

Tue **1**

---

Wed **2**

## March 2022

Thu **3**



Fri **4**

Sat **5**

Sun **6**

# March 2022

Mon **7**

Tue **8**

Wed **9**

March 2022

Thu **10**

| **March 2022** | | | | | | |
|---|---|---|---|---|---|---|
| M | T | W | T | F | S | **S** |
|  | 1 | 2 | 3 | 4 | 5 | **6** |
| 7 | 8 | 9 | 10 | 11 | 12 | **13** |
| 14 | 15 | 16 | 17 | 18 | 19 | **20** |
| 21 | 22 | 23 | 24 | 25 | 26 | **27** |
| 28 | 29 | 30 | 31 |  |  | |

Fri **11**

Sat **12**

Sun **13**

March 2022

Mon **14**

Tue **15**

Wed **16**

| March 2022 | | | | | | |
|---|---|---|---|---|---|---|
| M | T | W | T | F | S | S |
| | 1 | 2 | 3 | 4 | 5 | 6 |
| 7 | 8 | 9 | 10 | 11 | 12 | 13 |
| 14 | 15 | 16 | 17 | 18 | 19 | 20 |
| 21 | 22 | 23 | 24 | 25 | 26 | 27 |
| 28 | 29 | 30 | 31 | | | |

Thu **17**

Fri **18**

Sat **19**

Sun **20**

Mon **21**

Tue **22**

Wed **23**

March 2022

Thu **24**

Fri **25**

Sat **26**

Sun **27**

| March 2022 | | | | | | |
|---|---|---|---|---|---|---|
| M | T | W | T | F | S | S |
|  | 1 | 2 | 3 | 4 | 5 | 6 |
| 7 | 8 | 9 | 10 | 11 | 12 | 13 |
| 14 | 15 | 16 | 17 | 18 | 19 | 20 |
| 21 | 22 | 23 | 24 | 25 | 26 | 27 |
| 28 | 29 | 30 | 31 |  |  |  |

Mon **28**

Tue **29**

Wed **30**

## March 2022

Thu **31**

| March 2022 | | | | | | |
|---|---|---|---|---|---|---|
| **M** | **T** | **W** | **T** | **F** | **S** | **S** |
|  | 1 | 2 | 3 | 4 | 5 | **6** |
| 7 | 8 | 9 | 10 | 11 | 12 | **13** |
| 14 | 15 | 16 | 17 | 18 | 19 | **20** |
| 21 | 22 | 23 | 24 | 25 | 26 | **27** |
| 28 | 29 | 30 | 31 |  |  |  |

………April 2022………

Fri **1**

Sat **2**

Sun **3**

Mon **4**

Tue **5**

Wed **6**

April 2022

Thu **7**

| April 2022 | | | | | | |
|---|---|---|---|---|---|---|
| M | T | W | T | F | S | S |
| | | | | 1 | 2 | **3** |
| 4 | 5 | 6 | 7 | 8 | 9 | **10** |
| 11 | 12 | 13 | 14 | 15 | 16 | **17** |
| 18 | 19 | 20 | 21 | 22 | 23 | **24** |
| 25 | 26 | 27 | 28 | 29 | 30 | |

Fri **8**

Sat **9**

Sun **10**

Mon **11**

Tue **12**

Wed **13**

April 2022

Thu **14**

Fri **15**

Sat **16**

Sun **17**

Mon **18**

Tue **19**

Wed **20**

April 2022

Thu **21**

| M | T | W | T | F | S | S |
|---|---|---|---|---|---|---|
| April 2022 | | | | | | |
|  |  |  |  | 1 | 2 | **3** |
| 4 | 5 | 6 | 7 | 8 | 9 | **10** |
| 11 | 12 | 13 | 14 | 15 | 16 | **17** |
| 18 | 19 | 20 | 21 | 22 | 23 | **24** |
| 25 | 26 | 27 | 28 | 29 | 30 |  |

Fri **22**

Sat **23**

Sun **24**

Mon **25**

Tue **26**

Wed **27**

April 2022

| | April 2022 | | | | | | |
|---|---|---|---|---|---|---|---|
| M | T | W | T | F | S | S |
| | | | | 1 | 2 | 3 |
| 4 | 5 | 6 | 7 | 8 | 9 | 10 |
| 11 | 12 | 13 | 14 | 15 | 16 | 17 |
| 18 | 19 | 20 | 21 | 22 | 23 | 24 |
| 25 | 26 | 27 | 28 | 29 | 30 | |

Thu **28**

Fri **29**

Sat **30**

....... May 2022 .....

Sun **1**

# May 2022

Mon **2**

Tue **3**

Wed **4**

## May 2022

| | May 2022 | | | | | |
| M | T | W | T | F | S | S |
|---|---|---|---|---|---|---|
| | | | | | | 1 |
| 2 | 3 | 4 | 5 | 6 | 7 | 8 |
| 9 | 10 | 11 | 12 | 13 | 14 | 15 |
| 16 | 17 | 18 | 19 | 20 | 21 | 22 |
| 23 | 24 | 25 | 26 | 27 | 28 | 29 |
| 30 | 31 | | | | | |

Thu **5**

Fri **6**

Sat **7**

Sun **8**

Mon **9**

Tue **10**

Wed **11**

May 2022



Thu **12**

Fri **13**

Sat **14**

Sun **15**

Mon **16**

Tue **17**

Wed **18**

May 2022

Thu **19**

<table>
<tr><td colspan="7" align="center">**May 2022**</td></tr>
<tr><td>M</td><td>T</td><td>W</td><td>T</td><td>F</td><td>S</td><td>S</td></tr>
<tr><td></td><td></td><td></td><td></td><td></td><td></td><td>1</td></tr>
<tr><td>2</td><td>3</td><td>4</td><td>5</td><td>6</td><td>7</td><td>8</td></tr>
<tr><td>9</td><td>10</td><td>11</td><td>12</td><td>13</td><td>14</td><td>15</td></tr>
<tr><td>16</td><td>17</td><td>18</td><td>19</td><td>20</td><td>21</td><td>22</td></tr>
<tr><td>23</td><td>24</td><td>25</td><td>26</td><td>27</td><td>28</td><td>29</td></tr>
<tr><td>30</td><td>31</td><td></td><td></td><td></td><td></td><td></td></tr>
</table>

Fri **20**

Sat **21**

Sun **22**

May 2022

Mon **23**

Tue **24**

Wed **25**

May 2022

Thu **26**

---

Fri **27**

---

Sat **28**

Sun **29**

| May 2022 | | | | | | |
|---|---|---|---|---|---|---|
| M | T | W | T | F | S | S |
|  |  |  |  |  |  | 1 |
| 2 | 3 | 4 | 5 | 6 | 7 | 8 |
| 9 | 10 | 11 | 12 | 13 | 14 | 15 |
| 16 | 17 | 18 | 19 | 20 | 21 | 22 |
| 23 | 24 | 25 | 26 | 27 | 28 | 29 |
| 30 | 31 |  |  |  |  |  |

May 2022



Mon **30**

Tue **31**

……. June 2022 ……

Wed **1**

## June 2022



| M | T | W | T | F | S | S |
|---|---|---|---|---|---|---|
|   |   | 1 | 2 | 3 | 4 | 5 |
| 6 | 7 | 8 | 9 | 10 | 11 | 12 |
| 13 | 14 | 15 | 16 | 17 | 18 | 19 |
| 20 | 21 | 22 | 23 | 24 | 25 | 26 |
| 27 | 28 | 29 | 30 |   |   |   |

Thu **2**

Fri **3**

Sat **4**

Sun **5**

June 2022

Mon **6**

Tue **7**

Wed **8**

June 2022

| | June 2022 | | | | | | |
|---|---|---|---|---|---|---|---|
| M | T | W | T | F | S | S |
| | | 1 | 2 | 3 | 4 | 5 |
| 6 | 7 | 8 | 9 | 10 | 11 | 12 |
| 13 | 14 | 15 | 16 | 17 | 18 | 19 |
| 20 | 21 | 22 | 23 | 24 | 25 | 26 |
| 27 | 28 | 29 | 30 | | | |

Thu **9**

Fri **10**

Sat **11**

Sun **12**

Mon **13**

---

Tue **14**

---

Wed **15**

June 2022

Thu **16**

Fri **17**

Sat **18**

Sun **19**

| June 2022 | | | | | | |
|---|---|---|---|---|---|---|
| M | T | W | T | F | S | S |
| | | 1 | 2 | 3 | 4 | 5 |
| 6 | 7 | 8 | 9 | 10 | 11 | 12 |
| 13 | 14 | 15 | 16 | 17 | 18 | 19 |
| 20 | 21 | 22 | 23 | 24 | 25 | 26 |
| 27 | 28 | 29 | 30 | | | |

Mon **20**

Tue **21**

Wed **22**

June 2022

| | June 2022 | | | | | |
| M | T | W | T | F | S | S |
|---|---|---|---|---|---|---|
| | | 1 | 2 | 3 | 4 | 5 |
| 6 | 7 | 8 | 9 | 10 | 11 | 12 |
| 13 | 14 | 15 | 16 | 17 | 18 | 19 |
| 20 | 21 | 22 | 23 | 24 | 25 | 26 |
| 27 | 28 | 29 | 30 | | | |

Thu **23**

Fri **24**

Sat **25**

Sun **26**

Mon **27**

Tue **28**

Wed **29**

June 2022

Thu **30**

| June 2022 | | | | | | |
|---|---|---|---|---|---|---|
| M | T | W | T | F | S | S |
|  |  | 1 | 2 | 3 | 4 | 5 |
| 6 | 7 | 8 | 9 | 10 | 11 | 12 |
| 13 | 14 | 15 | 16 | 17 | 18 | 19 |
| 20 | 21 | 22 | 23 | 24 | 25 | 26 |
| 27 | 28 | 29 | 30 |  |  |  |

# Key dates

January

February

March

April

May

June

# Key dates

July

August

September

October

November

December

# CURRENT YEAR 2021

## January 2021

| M | T | W | T | F | S | S |
|---|---|---|---|---|---|---|
|  |  |  |  | 1 | 2 | 3 |
| 4 | 5 | 6 | 7 | 8 | 9 | 10 |
| 11 | 12 | 13 | 14 | 15 | 16 | 17 |
| 18 | 19 | 20 | 21 | 22 | 23 | 24 |
| 25 | 26 | 27 | 28 | 29 | 30 | 31 |

## February 2021

| M | T | W | T | F | S | S |
|---|---|---|---|---|---|---|
| 1 | 2 | 3 | 4 | 5 | 6 | 7 |
| 8 | 9 | 10 | 11 | 12 | 13 | 14 |
| 15 | 16 | 17 | 18 | 19 | 20 | 21 |
| 22 | 23 | 24 | 25 | 26 | 27 | 28 |

## March 2021

| M | T | W | T | F | S | S |
|---|---|---|---|---|---|---|
| 1 | 2 | 3 | 4 | 5 | 6 | 7 |
| 8 | 9 | 10 | 11 | 12 | 13 | 14 |
| 15 | 16 | 17 | 18 | 19 | 20 | 21 |
| 22 | 23 | 24 | 25 | 26 | 27 | 28 |
| 29 | 30 | 31 |  |  |  |  |

## April 2021

| M | T | W | T | F | S | S |
|---|---|---|---|---|---|---|
|  |  |  | 1 | 2 | 3 | 4 |
| 5 | 6 | 7 | 8 | 9 | 10 | 11 |
| 12 | 13 | 14 | 15 | 16 | 17 | 18 |
| 19 | 20 | 21 | 22 | 23 | 24 | 25 |
| 26 | 27 | 28 | 29 | 30 |  |  |

## May 2021

| M | T | W | T | F | S | S |
|---|---|---|---|---|---|---|
|  |  |  |  |  | 1 | 2 |
| 3 | 4 | 5 | 6 | 7 | 8 | 9 |
| 10 | 11 | 12 | 13 | 14 | 15 | 16 |
| 17 | 18 | 19 | 20 | 21 | 22 | 23 |
| 24 | 25 | 26 | 27 | 28 | 29 | 30 |
| 31 |  |  |  |  |  |  |

## June 2021

| M | T | W | T | F | S | S |
|---|---|---|---|---|---|---|
|  | 1 | 2 | 3 | 4 | 5 | 6 |
| 7 | 8 | 9 | 10 | 11 | 12 | 13 |
| 14 | 15 | 16 | 17 | 18 | 19 | 20 |
| 21 | 22 | 23 | 24 | 25 | 26 | 27 |
| 28 | 29 | 30 |  |  |  |  |

## July 2021

| M | T | W | T | F | S | S |
|---|---|---|---|---|---|---|
|  |  |  | 1 | 2 | 3 | 4 |
| 5 | 6 | 7 | 8 | 9 | 10 | 11 |
| 12 | 13 | 14 | 15 | 16 | 17 | 18 |
| 19 | 20 | 21 | 22 | 23 | 24 | 25 |
| 26 | 27 | 28 | 29 | 30 | 31 |  |

## August 2021

| M | T | W | T | F | S | S |
|---|---|---|---|---|---|---|
|  |  |  |  |  |  | 1 |
| 2 | 3 | 4 | 5 | 6 | 7 | 8 |
| 9 | 10 | 11 | 12 | 13 | 14 | 15 |
| 16 | 17 | 18 | 19 | 20 | 21 | 22 |
| 23 | 24 | 25 | 26 | 27 | 28 | 29 |
| 30 | 31 |  |  |  |  |  |

## September 2021

| M | T | W | T | F | S | S |
|---|---|---|---|---|---|---|
|  |  | 1 | 2 | 3 | 4 | 5 |
| 6 | 7 | 8 | 9 | 10 | 11 | 12 |
| 13 | 14 | 15 | 16 | 17 | 18 | 19 |
| 20 | 21 | 22 | 23 | 24 | 25 | 26 |
| 27 | 28 | 29 | 30 |  |  |  |

## October 2021

| M | T | W | T | F | S | S |
|---|---|---|---|---|---|---|
|  |  |  |  | 1 | 2 | 3 |
| 4 | 5 | 6 | 7 | 8 | 9 | 10 |
| 11 | 12 | 13 | 14 | 15 | 16 | 17 |
| 18 | 19 | 20 | 21 | 22 | 23 | 24 |
| 25 | 26 | 27 | 28 | 29 | 30 | 31 |

## November 2021

| M | T | W | T | F | S | S |
|---|---|---|---|---|---|---|
| 1 | 2 | 3 | 4 | 5 | 6 | 7 |
| 8 | 9 | 10 | 11 | 12 | 13 | 14 |
| 15 | 16 | 17 | 18 | 19 | 20 | 21 |
| 22 | 23 | 24 | 25 | 26 | 27 | 28 |
| 29 | 30 |  |  |  |  |  |

## December 2021

| M | T | W | T | F | S | S |
|---|---|---|---|---|---|---|
|  |  | 1 | 2 | 3 | 4 | 5 |
| 6 | 7 | 8 | 9 | 10 | 11 | 12 |
| 13 | 14 | 15 | 16 | 17 | 18 | 19 |
| 20 | 21 | 22 | 23 | 24 | 25 | 26 |
| 27 | 28 | 29 | 30 | 31 |  |  |

2021

# CURRENT  YEAR 2021

## January 2022

| M | T | W | T | F | S | S |
|---|---|---|---|---|---|---|
|  |  |  |  |  |  | 1 | 2 |
| 3 | 4 | 5 | 6 | 7 | 8 | 9 |
| 10 | 11 | 12 | 13 | 14 | 15 | 16 |
| 17 | 18 | 19 | 20 | 21 | 22 | 23 |
| 24 | 25 | 26 | 27 | 28 | 29 | 30 |
| 31 |  |  |  |  |  |  |

## February 2022

| M | T | W | T | F | S | S |
|---|---|---|---|---|---|---|
|  | 1 | 2 | 3 | 4 | 5 | 6 |
| 7 | 8 | 9 | 10 | 11 | 12 | 13 |
| 14 | 15 | 16 | 17 | 18 | 19 | 20 |
| 21 | 22 | 23 | 24 | 25 | 26 | 27 |
| 28 |  |  |  |  |  |  |

## March 2022

| M | T | W | T | F | S | S |
|---|---|---|---|---|---|---|
|  | 1 | 2 | 3 | 4 | 5 | 6 |
| 7 | 8 | 9 | 10 | 11 | 12 | 13 |
| 14 | 15 | 16 | 17 | 18 | 19 | 20 |
| 21 | 22 | 23 | 24 | 25 | 26 | 27 |
| 28 | 29 | 30 | 31 |  |  |  |

## April 2022

| M | T | W | T | F | S | S |
|---|---|---|---|---|---|---|
|  |  |  |  | 1 | 2 | 3 |
| 4 | 5 | 6 | 7 | 8 | 9 | 10 |
| 11 | 12 | 13 | 14 | 15 | 16 | 17 |
| 18 | 19 | 20 | 21 | 22 | 23 | 24 |
| 25 | 26 | 27 | 28 | 29 | 30 |  |

## May 2022

| M | T | W | T | F | S | S |
|---|---|---|---|---|---|---|
|  |  |  |  |  |  | 1 |
| 2 | 3 | 4 | 5 | 6 | 7 | 8 |
| 9 | 10 | 11 | 12 | 13 | 14 | 15 |
| 16 | 17 | 18 | 19 | 20 | 21 | 22 |
| 23 | 24 | 25 | 26 | 27 | 28 | 29 |
| 30 | 31 |  |  |  |  |  |

## June 2022

| M | T | W | T | F | S | S |
|---|---|---|---|---|---|---|
|  |  | 1 | 2 | 3 | 4 | 5 |
| 6 | 7 | 8 | 9 | 10 | 11 | 12 |
| 13 | 14 | 15 | 16 | 17 | 18 | 19 |
| 20 | 21 | 22 | 23 | 24 | 25 | 26 |
| 27 | 28 | 29 | 30 |  |  |  |

## July 2022

| M | T | W | T | F | S | S |
|---|---|---|---|---|---|---|
|  |  |  |  | 1 | 2 | 3 |
| 4 | 5 | 6 | 7 | 8 | 9 | 10 |
| 11 | 12 | 13 | 14 | 15 | 16 | 17 |
| 18 | 19 | 20 | 21 | 22 | 23 | 24 |
| 25 | 26 | 27 | 28 | 29 | 30 | 31 |

## August 2022

| M | T | W | T | F | S | S |
|---|---|---|---|---|---|---|
| 1 | 2 | 3 | 4 | 5 | 6 | 7 |
| 8 | 9 | 10 | 11 | 12 | 13 | 14 |
| 15 | 16 | 17 | 18 | 19 | 20 | 21 |
| 22 | 23 | 24 | 25 | 26 | 27 | 28 |
| 29 | 30 | 31 |  |  |  |  |

## September 2022

| M | T | W | T | F | S | S |
|---|---|---|---|---|---|---|
|  |  |  | 1 | 2 | 3 | 4 |
| 5 | 6 | 7 | 8 | 9 | 10 | 11 |
| 12 | 13 | 14 | 15 | 16 | 17 | 18 |
| 19 | 20 | 21 | 22 | 23 | 24 | 25 |
| 26 | 27 | 28 | 29 | 30 |  |  |

## October 2022

| M | T | W | T | F | S | S |
|---|---|---|---|---|---|---|
|  |  |  |  |  | 1 | 2 |
| 3 | 4 | 5 | 6 | 7 | 8 | 9 |
| 10 | 11 | 12 | 13 | 14 | 15 | 16 |
| 17 | 18 | 19 | 20 | 21 | 22 | 23 |
| 24 | 25 | 26 | 27 | 28 | 29 | 30 |
| 31 |  |  |  |  |  |  |

## November 2022

| M | T | W | T | F | S | S |
|---|---|---|---|---|---|---|
|  | 1 | 2 | 3 | 4 | 5 | 6 |
| 7 | 8 | 9 | 10 | 11 | 12 | 13 |
| 14 | 15 | 16 | 17 | 18 | 19 | 20 |
| 21 | 22 | 23 | 24 | 25 | 26 | 27 |
| 28 | 29 | 30 |  |  |  |  |

## December 2022

| M | T | W | T | F | S | S |
|---|---|---|---|---|---|---|
|  |  |  | 1 | 2 | 3 | 4 |
| 5 | 6 | 7 | 8 | 9 | 10 | 11 |
| 12 | 13 | 14 | 15 | 16 | 17 | 18 |
| 19 | 20 | 21 | 22 | 23 | 24 | 25 |
| 26 | 27 | 28 | 29 | 30 | 31 |  |

2022